Embracing Liberation: Navigating the Journey to True Freedom

Leadership, Empowerment, and Social Change in Today's World

Chapters

Embracing Liberation" is a comprehensive exploration of the journey towards true freedom, encompassing themes of leadership, empowerment, and social change.

From uncovering the legacy of historical oppression to examining the psychology of control and fear, the book delves into the complexities of modern-day power dynamics and their impact on individuals and communities.

Through practical tools and strategies, readers are empowered to cultivate authentic leadership, foster inclusive cultures, and drive positive change in the world.

As the book culminates in a call to action, readers are inspired to embark on their own journey towards true liberation, guided by the principles of authenticity, courage, and collective action.

Embracing Liberation: Navigating the Journey to True Freedom" is a profound exploration of leadership, empowerment, and social change in today's world. This book takes readers on a transformative journey, unraveling the complexities of historical oppression, ideological slavery, and the psychology of control. Through practical insights and actionable strategies, readers are equipped to cu tivate authentic leadership, foster inclusive cultures, and drive positive change in their lives and communities.

Designed for individuals seeking to deepen their understanding of power dynamics and societal impact, "Embracing Liberation" offers a roadmap for personal and collective transformation. Whether you're a seasoned leader, a budding activist, or simply someone passionate about creating a more just and equitable world, this book provides invaluable guidance and inspiration.

The impact of "Embracing Liberation" extends far beyond its pages, sparkirg conversations, fostering collaboration, and igniting movements for social change. By empowering readers to embrace their authenticity, challenge oppression, and take inspired action, this book has the potential to catalyze meaningful progress towards a more compassionate, inclusive, and liberated society.

Join us on this journey towards true freedom – where courage, resilience, and collective action pave the way for a brighter, more equitable future for all. "Embracing Liberation" is not just a book – it's a call to action, an invitation to rise up, and a roadmap for building a world where every individual can thrive and flourish in dignity and freedom

Chapter 1: The Legacy of Historical Oppression

Have you ever wondered how the shadows of the past continue to shape the contours of our present reality?

To understand the complexities of modern-day oppression, we must first unravel the threads of history that weave through the fabric of our collective consciousness.

This chapter delves deep into the annals of time, exploring the enduring legacy of historical oppression and its profound impact on contemporary society.

From the ancient civilizations of Mesopotamia to the empires of Rome and beyond, systems of oppression have plagued humanity for millennia.

Whether manifested through chattel slavery, feudal serfdom, or caste systems, the specter of domination and subjugation has cast a long shadow over successive generations.

But what are the lasting effects of these oppressive regimes, and how do they continue to reverberate in our modern world?

Scientific research corroborates what history has long attested: trauma leaves an indelible mark on the human psyche, transcending generations and permeating societal structures. Studies in epigenetics reveal how the experiences of our ancestors can influence our genetic expression, predisposing us to certain behavioral patterns and vulnerabilities. Could it be that the trauma of past oppression lingers in our DNA, shaping our attitudes, beliefs, and interpersonal relationships?

Moreover, the legacy of historical oppression extends far beyond the realm of genetics, permeating the cultural, economic, and political landscapes of contemporary society.

Consider the enduring disparities in wealth and opportunity between historically marginalized communities and their privileged counterparts. From the enduring wealth gap between white and Black Americans to the caste-based inequalities in India, the echoes of past injustice resonate in present-day social hierarchies.

But perhaps most insidious of all is the psychological legacy of historical oppression, which manifests in internalized feelings of inferiority, shame, and self-doubt.

Generations of subjugated peoples have internalized the narratives of their oppressors, perpetuating cycles of self-sabotage and intergenerational trauma. How do we break free from the psychological chains of our ancestors and reclaim our inherent worth and dignity?

Yet, amidst the darkness of oppression, there is also resilience, resistance, and the indomitable spirit of human perseverance.

Throughout history, oppressed peoples have risen up against their oppressors, challenging the status quo and demanding justice, equality, and freedom. From the abolitionist movements of the 19th century to the civil rights struggles of the 20th century and beyond, the arc of history bends towards justice when individuals unite in solidarity and courage.

As we reflect on the legacy of historical oppression, we are confronted with a choice: to perpetuate the cycles of injustice and subjugation or to break free from the chains of the past and forge a new path towards liberation.

It is incumbent upon each of us to confront the uncomfortable truths of history, to acknowledge the privileges bestowed upon some at the expense of others, and to work towards a more just and equitable future for all.

In the words of Maya Angelou, "History, despite its wrenching pain, cannot be unlived, but if faced with courage, need not be lived again." Let us face the legacy of historical oppression with courage and determination, knowing that our actions today have the power to shape a brighter tomorrow for generations to come.

Reflection: As we journey through the annals of history, we are confronted with the profound impact of past oppression on our present reality.

Yet, within the depths of darkness, there also lies the seeds of resilience, resistance, and hope. May we heed the lessons of the past and strive towards a future where justice, equality, and freedom reign supreme.

Chapter 2: Unmasking Ideological Slavery

As we peel back the layers of history, we uncover the insidious legacy of oppression that continues to cast its shadow over our modern world. Yet, the chains of bondage are not always forged from iron; often, they are woven from the fabric of ideology, shaping our thoughts, beliefs, and behaviors in subtle yet profound ways.

In this chapter, we embark on a journey to unmask the hidden mechanisms of ideological slavery, illuminating the ways in which it manifests in our daily lives and perpetuates systemic inequalities.

Consider, for example, the pervasive influence of consumer culture in our society. From an early age, we are bombarded with messages that equate happiness and fulfillment with material possessions.

Advertisements promise us that if only we buy this product or own that gadget, we will finally be complete. Yet, beneath the veneer of consumerism lies a deeper truth: our worth as individuals cannot be measured by the things we possess.

Scriptural wisdom reminds us that "a person's life does not consist in the abundance of their possessions" (Luke 12:15). Indeed, true freedom is found not in the accumulation of material wealth, but in the cultivation of inner richness and spiritual abundance.

When we become slaves to consumerism, we relinquish our autonomy and agency, allowing external forces to dictate our desires and shape our identities.

Moreover, ideological slavery extends beyond the realm of consumer culture, permeating every facet of our lives, from our relationships to our work environments.

Consider the insidious ways in which toxic ideologies such as racism, sexism, and classism continue to exert their influence, shaping our perceptions of ourselves and others. When we internalize these ideologies, we become complicit in perpetuating systems of oppression, even if unwittingly.

Historical proverbs caution us that "those who do not learn from history are doomed to repeat it." Indeed, the echoes of past injustices reverberate through the corridors of power, reminding us of the dangers of complacency and conformity.

Yet, there is hope in the power of awareness and enlightenment. By shining a light on the hidden mechanisms of ideological slavery, we can begin to dismantle the systems of oppression that ensnare us and forge a path towards genuine liberation.

Reflective insight invites us to interrogate the narratives that have been handed down to us and to challenge the status quo.

When we question the underlying assumptions and beliefs that govern our lives, we reclaim our agency and autonomy, charting a course towards a more just and equitable future. In the words of Nelson Mandela, "to be free is not merely to cast off one's chains, but to live in a way that respects and enhances the freedom of others."

As we navigate the complexities of ideological slavery, let us remember that true freedom begins within. When we cultivate a sense of inner richness and spiritual abundance, we transcend the limitations of external circumstances and find liberation in the depths of our own souls.

May we have the courage to unmask the chains of ideological slavery and embark on a journey towards a more just, equitable, and compassionate world for all.

Transition to Chapter 3: As we peel back the layers of ideological slavery, we confront the uncomfortable truths that lie beneath the surface of our society.

In the next chapter, we delve deeper into the psychology of control, exploring the dynamics of fear and freedom in shaping our thoughts, behaviors, and relationships. Join us as we embark on a journey to understand the subtle yet profound ways in which fear influences our lives and inhibits our ability to live authentically and fully.

Chapter 3: The Psychology of Control: Fear Versus Freedom

As we journey deeper into the labyrinth of ideological slavery, we encounter the intricate interplay between the psychology of control, fear, and freedom.

At the heart of this dynamic lies a fundamental question: are we driven by fear or guided by the pursuit of authentic freedom? In this chapter, we unravel the complexities of human psychology, exploring how the specter of fear shapes our thoughts, behaviors, and relationships, while also illuminating the path towards genuine liberation.

Consider, for a moment, the pervasive influence of fear in our daily lives. From the fear of failure to the fear of rejection, from the fear of the unknown to the fear of change, fear exerts a powerful grip on our consciousness, dictating the choices we make and the paths we pursue. But what lies at the root of this pervasive sense of fear, and how does it manifest in our thoughts and behaviors?

Psychological research suggests that fear is often rooted in a primal instinct for self-preservation, wired into our brains as a means of avoiding danger and ensuring our survival.

Yet, in the modern world, many of the fears that grip us are not immediate threats to our physical well-being but rather perceived threats to our ego, our identity, or our sense of security. How do we distinguish between legitimate fears that serve to protect us and irrational fears that hold us back from realizing our full potential?

Moreover, the psychology of control reveals how fear can be wielded as a tool of manipulation and oppression by those in positions of power.

Whether through subtle forms of coercion or overt displays of authority, fear-based tactics are often employed to maintain social order and uphold existing power structures. But at what cost do we sacrifice our autonomy and agency in exchange for the illusion of safety and security?

Yet, amidst the shadows of fear, there also shines the beacon of freedom – the innate human desire to break free from the shackles of oppression and live authentically and fully.

In the words of Franklin D. Roosevelt, "the only thing we have to fear is fear itself." When we confront our fears with courage and resilience, we reclaim our power and chart a course towards genuine liberation.

Practical examples abound in our daily lives, from the employee who stays in a toxic job out of fear of financial insecurity to the individual who suppresses their true identity for fear of societal judgment.

How do these examples reflect the psychology of control, and what steps can we take to transcend the grip of fear and embrace our inherent freedom?

Reflective insight invites us to question the narratives that perpetuate fear and oppression, to challenge the status quo, and to envision a future where authenticity, autonomy, and empowerment reign supreme.

When we cultivate a mindset of courage, resilience, and self-awareness, we transcend the limitations of fear and forge a path towards a more just, equitable, and compassionate world for all.

As we navigate the complexities of the psychology of control, let us remember that true freedom begins within – within the depths of our own consciousness, within the recesses of our own hearts. When we confront our fears with courage and compassion, we unlock the door to genuine liberation and embark on a journey towards a brighter, more hopeful future for ourselves and for generations to come.

Transition to Chapter 4: As we peel back the layers of fear and control, we confront the fundamental question of motivations behind our actions: are we driven by intrinsic desires or extrinsic pressures? Join us in the next chapter as we explore the dynamic interplay between intrinsic and extrinsic motivations and their profound implications for our pursuit of freedom and fulfillment.

Chapter 4: Motivations Behind the Mask: Intrinsic vs. Extrinsic

"What drives us to action: the whispers of our innermost desires or the clamor of external expectations?"

The ancient proverb "Know thyself" beckons us to journey inward, uncovering the motivations that propel us forward in our quest for fulfillment and meaning. In this chapter, we explore the intricate interplay between intrinsic and extrinsic motivations, and their profound implications for authenticity and freedom.

At the heart of this exploration lies a fundamental question: what truly motivates us to act? Are our actions driven by a deep-seated desire for personal growth, fulfillment, and self-expression (intrinsic motivation), or are we merely responding to external rewards, pressures, and social norms (extrinsic motivation)?

Intrinsic motivations stem from the inherent pleasure and satisfaction derived from engaging in an activity for its own sake. Think of the artist who paints for the sheer joy of self-expression, or the athlete who competes for the love of the game. Intrinsic motivations are rooted in authenticity, autonomy, and purpose, fueling our endeavors with passion and meaning.

Conversely, extrinsic motivations arise from external sources such as rewards, recognition, or social approval.

Consider the student who studies diligently to please their parents or earn high grades. While extrinsic motivations may yield short-term benefits, they often come at the expense of personal autonomy and intrinsic satisfaction, leading to feelings of emptiness and disillusionment.

Psychological research suggests that intrinsic motivations are inherently more sustainable and fulfilling than extrinsic motivations.

When we align our actions with our values and passions, we experience a profound sense of flow – a state of effortless immersion and focus where our sense of self expands. Intrinsic motivations nourish our souls, igniting the spark of creativity, curiosity, and joy within us.

Yet, societal conditioning and external pressures can often overshadow our intrinsic desires, leading us to prioritize external rewards and validation. How do we navigate the tension between external expectations and internal convictions, and cultivate a life guided by authenticity and purpose?

Reflective insight invites us to examine the stories we tell ourselves about success, happiness, and fulfillment. When we peel back the layers of societal conditioning, we uncover the seeds of our deepest aspirations and dreams. What are the whispers of our innermost desires, and how can we nurture them into fruition?

Historical and cultural references offer valuable insights into the timeless quest for authenticity and self-discovery. From ancient philosophers to indigenous traditions, diverse voices remind us of the importance of living in alignment with our true nature and values.

As we navigate the complexities of intrinsic and extrinsic motivations, let us remember that true freedom begins within – within the depths of our own hearts and minds.

When we honor our intrinsic desires and cultivate a life guided by authenticity and purpose, we unlock the door to genuine fulfillment and embark on a journey towards a more meaningful existence.

Chapter 5: Rebellion in Disguise, Misconduct as a Manifestation

As we delve deeper into the intricate interplay of motivations, we encounter a phenomenon where rebellion takes on various forms, often masquerading as misconduct.

In this chapter, we unravel the complexities of rebellion in disguise, exploring how misconduct serves as a manifestation of deeper underlying issues, and how understanding these dynamics can lead to transformative insights and growth.

Imagine a scenario where an employee consistently arrives late to work, misses deadlines, and displays a lack of engagement in their tasks. At first glance, these behaviors may appear as mere acts of negligence or irresponsibility. However, upon closer examination, we may uncover a deeper layer of discontent, frustration, or disconnection from their work environment.

Rebellion in disguise often arises when individuals feel stifled, undervalued, or marginalized within their organizations. Perhaps the employee in question feels unfulfilled in their role, lacks opportunities for growth and advancement, or experiences interpersonal conflicts with colleagues or superiors.

Instead of voicing their concerns openly, they resort to passive-aggressive behaviors or acts of defiance as a means of asserting their autonomy and reclaiming a sense of agency.

Misconduct, therefore, serves as a manifestation of unmet needs, unresolved conflicts, or systemic injustices within the workplace. It is a symptom of deeper underlying issues that demand attention and resolution.

By reframing misconduct as a call for help rather than a mere transgression, organizations can adopt a more compassionate and proactive approach to addressing these challenges.

Consider another example where a student constantly disrupts class, exhibits disruptive behavior, and fails to comply with academic standards. While it may be tempting to attribute these actions to a lack of discipline or respect for authority, a deeper exploration may reveal underlying factors such as learning disabilities, trauma, or social-emotional challenges.

In such cases, rebellion in disguise manifests as a cry for support, understanding, and accommodation. Instead of resorting to punitive measures or disciplinary actions, educators can adopt a trauma-informed approach that seeks to address the root causes of misconduct and provide the necessary support and resources for students to thrive.

Moreover, rebellion in disguise is not limited to individual behaviors but can also manifest at the systemic level within organizations and institutions.

Consider the #MeToo movement, where individuals across various industries spoke out against systemic sexism, harassment, and abuse of power.

What initially appeared as isolated incidents of misconduct revealed deeper patterns of systemic injustice and discrimination that permeated organizational cultures and power structures.

By recognizing and addressing rebellion in disguise, organizations can create environments that foster transparency, trust, and accountability. Instead of perpetuating cycles of repression and retaliation, they can cultivate cultures of open communication, empathy, and mutual respect.

This requires a willingness to listen, learn, and confront uncomfortable truths, even when they challenge existing power dynamics and entrenched norms.

In our personal lives, rebellion in disguise may manifest as patterns of self-sabotage, self-destructive behaviors, or relational conflicts. Perhaps we find ourselves engaging in substance abuse, excessive spending, or unhealthy relationships as a means of coping with underlying feelings of inadequacy, insecurity, or unresolved trauma.

By acknowledging and addressing these underlying issues with compassion and self-awareness, we can break free from the cycle of rebellion and reclaim our agency and autonomy.

This requires a willingness to confront our fears, insecurities, and vulnerabilities with honesty and vulnerability, and seek support and guidance from trusted allies, mentors, or therapists.

Ultimately, rebellion in disguise offers an opportunity for growth, healing, and transformation. It invites us to explore the deeper layers of our psyche, confront the shadows of our past, and reclaim our power and authenticity.

By embracing rebellion as a catalyst for change rather than a threat to be suppressed, we can embark on a journey towards greater self-awareness, resilience, and liberation.

Chapter 6: The Employer-Employee Divide, Bridging the Gap

"How do we bridge the chasm between employer and employee, forging connections built on trust, respect, and collaboration?"

In this chapter, we embark on a journey to unravel the complexities of the employer-employee relationship, exploring the divide that often separates these two entities and illuminating pathways towards bridging the gap.

Our intent is to foster greater understanding, empathy, and cooperation between employers and employees, creating environments where both parties can thrive and succeed.

At the heart of the employer-employee relationship lies a fundamental tension between power and vulnerability. Employers hold the reins of authority, dictating the terms of employment, setting expectations, and making decisions that impact the livelihoods of their employees.

On the other hand, employees depend on their employers for wages, benefits, and opportunities for growth and advancement.

This inherent power dynamic can breed mistrust, resentment, and disengagement if left unaddressed. Employees may feel undervalued, exploited, or disempowered, while employers may perceive their employees as mere cogs in the machinery of production, devoid of individual agency or intrinsic worth. How do we bridge this divide and cultivate relationships based on mutual respect, transparency, and collaboration?

One key to bridging the gap lies in fostering open communication and dialogue between employers and employees.

Too often, communication breakdowns occur when assumptions go unchallenged, grievances go unaddressed, and feedback goes unheard.

Employers must create channels for employees to voice their concerns, share their perspectives, and contribute to decision-making processes.

Likewise, employees must be willing to engage in constructive dialogue, express their needs and aspirations, and offer solutions to organizational challenges.

Transparency is another essential ingredient in bridging the employer–employee divide. When employers are transparent about their goals, values, and decision-making processes, employees feel a greater sense of trust and accountability.

Transparency fosters a culture of honesty, integrity, and shared responsibility, where both employers and employees are empowered to work towards common objectives with clarity and purpose.

Moreover, fostering a culture of empathy and understanding is crucial in bridging the gap between employers and employees.

Too often, employers may overlook the personal struggles, challenges, and aspirations of their employees, viewing them solely through the lens of productivity and performance.

By taking the time to listen, empathize, and support their employees on a human level, employers can cultivate a sense of belonging, loyalty, and commitment that transcends the transactional nature of the employer–employee relationship.

On the flip side, employees must also strive to understand the perspectives and constraints of their employers. Running a business entails myriad challenges, from financial pressures to market competition to regulatory compliance.

By empathizing with the complexities of their employer's role and demonstrating a willingness to collaborate and problem-solve, employees can foster a culture of partnership and cooperation that benefits both parties.

Bridging the employer-employee divide requires a willingness to challenge entrenched norms, biases, and power dynamics that perpetuate inequality and division.

It requires a commitment to equity, fairness, and inclusion, where all individuals are valued and respected for their unique contributions and perspectives. How do we create workplaces where diversity is celebrated, dissent is welcomed, and collaboration is the norm?

In conclusion, bridging the gap between employers and employees is not merely a matter of policy or procedure; it is a fundamental shift in mindset and culture.

It requires humility, empathy, and a willingness to listen and learn from one another. By cultivating relationships based on trust, transparency, and collaboration, we can create workplaces where both employers and employees thrive, innovate, and succeed together.

How can we each contribute to bridging the divide in our own spheres of influence, and what steps can we take to create a more equitable and inclusive future for all?

Chapter 7: Cultivating a Culture of Respect and Dignity

"Respect for ourselves guides our morals, respect for others guides our manners.' - Laurence Sterne

In this chapter, we delve into the essential components of cultivating a culture of respect and dignity within organizations and communities. Drawing from insights gained in previous chapters, we explore practical strategies for fostering environments where every individual is valued, heard, and treated with dignity and respect.

At the core of cultivating a culture of respect and dignity lies a recognition of the inherent worth and humanity of every individual. Regardless of differences in background, experience, or perspective, each person deserves to be treated with dignity, kindness, and empathy.

As we reflect on the dynamics of power, privilege, and oppression discussed in earlier chapters, we understand the importance of dismantling systems and behaviors that perpetuate inequality and discrimination.

One key aspect of cultivating a culture of respect and dignity is fostering empathy and understanding among members of the community. Empathy allows us to step into the shoes of others, to see the world through their eyes, and to recognize their struggles, joys, and aspirations as our own.

By actively listening to the stories and experiences of others, we can bridge divides, build connections, and cultivate a sense of belonging and solidarity.

Moreover, cultivating a culture of respect and dignity requires creating spaces where diverse voices are heard, valued, and respected.

Too often, marginalized individuals and communities are silenced or overlooked, their perspectives dismissed or invalidated.

By actively seeking out and amplifying marginalized voices, we create more inclusive and equitable environments where everyone has the opportunity to contribute and thrive.

Reflecting on the employer-employee relationship discussed in previous chapters, we recognize the importance of fostering mutual respect and collaboration in the workplace.

Employers must lead by example, modeling respectful behavior and creating policies and practices that prioritize the well-being and dignity of their employees. By valuing the contributions and perspectives of their employees, employers foster a culture of trust, loyalty, and commitment that benefits both parties.

Employees, in turn, must also cultivate respect and dignity in their interactions with colleagues and superiors.

This requires treating others with kindness, empathy, and professionalism, regardless of differences in opinion or background.

By fostering a culture of respect and collaboration, employees contribute to a positive and inclusive work environment where everyone feels valued and respected.

Practical strategies for cultivating a culture of respect and dignity include implementing training programs on diversity, equity, and inclusion, establishing clear policies and procedures for addressing discrimination and harassment, and fostering open communication and dialogue among members of the community.

Additionally, organizations can create opportunities for employees to participate in decision-making processes and provide feedback on issues that impact their lives and livelihoods.

Reflecting on the themes of rebellion in disguise and the employer-employee divide discussed in earlier chapters, we understand that cultivating a culture of respect and dignity is not merely a matter of superficial gestures or tokenism.

It requires a fundamental shift in mindset and behavior. It requires a commitment to empathy, humility, and continuous learning, where everyone is willing to challenge their own biases and assumptions and actively work towards creating a more just and equitable world for all.

In conclusion, cultivating a culture of respect and dignity is a collective responsibility that requires the active participation and commitment of every individual within the organization or community.

By fostering empathy, understanding, and collaboration, we can create environments where everyone feels valued, heard, and respected. How can we each contribute to cultivating a culture of respect and dignity in our own spheres of influence, and what steps can we take to create a more inclusive and equitable future for all?

Chapter 8: From Coercion to Collaboration, Redefining Power Dynamics

Imagine a mighty tree standing tall in a forest, its branches reaching towards the sky, its roots digging deep into the earth. For centuries, this tree has thrived, its strength and resilience a testament to the power of nature.

Yet, upon closer inspection, we discover that this tree is not a solitary entity but part of a vast interconnected network of life, where each leaf, each twig, each root plays a vital role in sustaining the whole.

Similarly, in our human interactions and organizations, power dynamics often resemble the towering tree, with individuals and institutions wielding authority and influence over others.

However, like the intricate ecosystem of the forest, true power lies not in domination or coercion but in collaboration and cooperation.

In this chapter, we explore the journey from coercion to collaboration, redefining power dynamics to create environments where all can flourish and thrive.

Reflecting on our exploration of rebellion in disguise and the employer–employee divide, we recognize that traditional power dynamics often breed resentment, mistrust, and disengagement.

When power is concentrated in the hands of a few, those on the margins are left feeling disempowered and voiceless. How can we shift from a model of power-over to a model of power-with, where all voices are valued and respected?

One key aspect of redefining power dynamics is fostering a culture of collaboration and shared decision-making. Instead of top-down directives and commands, organizations can embrace participatory processes that empower all members to contribute their ideas, insights, and expertise.

By involving stakeholders in decision-making processes, organizations tap into the collective wisdom and creativity of the entire community, leading to more innovative solutions and better outcomes for all.

Moreover, redefining power dynamics requires a willingness to challenge traditional hierarchies and structures that perpetuate inequality and exclusion.

Just as the mighty tree relies on its roots, that are both large and small, singular and yet intricately intertwined to anchor and sustain it, organizations must create strong foundations of trust, respect, and mutual accountability.

This means dismantling barriers to participation, amplifying marginalized voices, and creating pathways for leadership and advancement for all members of the community.

Consideration of the employer-employee relationship sheds light on the importance of cultivating relationships based on trust, respect, and collaboration. Instead of viewing employees as mere resources to be exploited, employers can recognize their intrinsic value and potential contributions to the organization.

By fostering a culture of empowerment and autonomy, employers empower their employees to take ownership of their work, innovate, and contribute to the collective success of the organization.

Employees, in turn, must also embrace their agency and responsibility in shaping the organizational culture.

By actively participating in decision-making processes, offering constructive feedback, and advocating for change, employees can challenge existing power dynamics and create more inclusive and equitable workplaces.

When power is shared and distributed among all members of the organization, everyone benefits from a sense of ownership, belonging, and purpose.

It is time to lift the corporate veil of inequity and unmask the pervasive isolation, the teeming stealth of hand, the subtle engineered machinations and facade that permeates the corridors of corporate offices, and society, and migrate towards systems that are amplified and sustained with equity, and just rewards, this must be our pulsating reality.

In reflecting on our journey from coercion to collaboration, we recognize that redefining power dynamics is not a linear process but a continuous journey of growth and transformation.

It requires humility, empathy, and a willingness to challenge the status quo in pursuit of a more just and equitable world. How can we each contribute to redefining power dynamics in our own spheres of influence, and what steps can we take to create a more collaborative and inclusive future for all?

Reflecting on the chapters preceding this, we see the threads of understanding and empathy weaving through our exploration.

As we continue to navigate the complexities of human relationships and organizational dynamics, may we remain committed to fostering cultures of respect, dignity, and collaboration, where every individual is valued and empowered to contribute their unique gifts to the greater good.

Chapter 9: Liberation Through Leadership, Embracing Authenticity

Picture a group of weary travelers trekking through a dense forest, their path obscured by thick foliage and tangled undergrowth. As they navigate the winding trails and treacherous terrain, they long for a guiding light to lead them out of the darkness and into the light.

Suddenly, amidst the shadows, a figure emerges – a beacon of hope and inspiration. This leader, unencumbered by pretense or facade, leads with authenticity and integrity, illuminating the path forward for all who follow.

In this chapter, we explore the transformative power of leadership rooted in authenticity – a leadership that liberates, empowers, and inspires others to reach their full potential.

Drawing from insights gained in previous chapters, we delve into the qualities and practices that define authentic leadership and the profound impact it has on individuals, organizations, and communities.

Authentic leadership is characterized by a deep sense of self-awareness and congruence between one's values, beliefs, and actions.

Authentic leaders are grounded in their identity and purpose, unafraid to embrace their vulnerabilities and imperfections.

They lead with transparency, honesty, and humility, forging genuine connections based on trust, respect, and empathy.

Consider the example of Nelson Mandela, whose unwavering commitment to justice and reconciliation inspired a nation and transformed the course of history.

Mandela's authenticity stemmed from his deep conviction in the inherent dignity and equality of all people, regardless of race or background. By leading with integrity and compassion, Mandela embodied the principles of authentic leadership, empowering others to join him in the fight for freedom and equality.

Authentic leaders also possess a keen sense of empathy and emotional intelligence, allowing them to connect with others on a deeper level and understand their perspectives and experiences. They listen with an open heart and mind, validating the feelings and concerns of those they lead.

By creating spaces for dialogue, collaboration, and shared decision-making, authentic leaders foster environments where everyone feels valued, heard, and respected.

Reflecting on our exploration of power dynamics and collaboration, we recognize that authentic leadership transcends traditional notions of authority and control. Instead of wielding power over others, authentic leaders empower and uplift those around them, unleashing the collective potential of the entire community.

They create cultures of inclusion, innovation, and belonging, where diversity is celebrated, dissent is welcomed, and collaboration is the norm.

Moreover, authentic leadership requires a willingness to embrace vulnerability and embrace uncertainty. In a world that often prizes certainty and invulnerability, authentic leaders are not afraid to admit their mistakes, acknowledge their limitations, and seek feedback and support from others. By modeling vulnerability and resilience, authentic leaders create environments where individuals feel safe to take risks, experiment, and grow.

Consideration of the employer–employee relationship sheds light on the transformative impact of authentic leadership in the workplace. Authentic leaders inspire trust, loyalty, and commitment among their employees, fostering a culture of engagement, creativity, and innovation.

Employees are more likely to go above and beyond their duties when they feel valued, respected, and empowered by their leaders.

Reflecting on our journey from coercion to collaboration, we recognize that authentic leadership is a catalyst for liberation and transformation.

It liberates individuals from the constraints of fear, conformity, and self-doubt, empowering them to step into their full potential and contribute their unique gifts to the world.

How can we each cultivate authentic leadership in our own lives and communities, and what impact can it have on the world around us?

As we continue to navigate the complexities of leadership and human relationships, may we remain committed to leading with authenticity, integrity, and compassion. May we strive to be the guiding lights that illuminate the path forward, inspiring others to embrace their authenticity and create a more just, equitable, and compassionate world for all.

Chapter 10: Beyond the Corporate Veil, Impacting Society at Large

"No man is an island, entire of itself; every man is a piece of the continent, a part of the main." - John Donne

In this chapter, we embark on a journey beyond the confines of corporate structures and organizational boundaries, exploring the profound impact that businesses and leaders can have on society at large.

Drawing from insights gleaned from previous chapters, we delve into the synergistic relationship between business, leadership, and societal impact, uncovering opportunities for positive change and transformation.

Reflecting on our exploration of authentic leadership and collaboration, we recognize that businesses and leaders wield immense influence not only within their own spheres of operation but also in shaping the broader social and economic landscape. Beyond maximizing profits and shareholder value, businesses have a moral and ethical responsibility to contribute to the well-being and prosperity of the communities they serve.

One key aspect of impacting society at large is embracing a stakeholder-centric approach to business, where the interests of all stakeholders – including employees, customers, suppliers, and the broader community – are taken into consideration.

By prioritizing social and environmental sustainability alongside financial performance, businesses can create value for society as a whole while also ensuring their long-term viability and success.

Consider the example of Patagonia, a leading outdoor apparel company known for its commitment to environmental stewardship and social responsibility. From investing in sustainable supply chains to advocating for environmental conservation.

Patagonia demonstrates how businesses can align their values with their actions to create positive change in the world.

By integrating purpose and profit, businesses like Patagonia inspire others to make reasonable and practical adjustments in order to be better positioned to contribute to a more sustainable and equitable future.

Moreover, impacting society at large requires businesses to actively engage with pressing social and environmental challenges, from climate change and inequality to poverty and injustice.

By leveraging their resources, expertise, and influence, businesses can drive meaningful progress and catalyze systemic change. Whether through philanthropy, advocacy, or innovative business practices, businesses have a unique opportunity to be agents of social change and transformation.

Reflecting on our exploration of power dynamics and collaboration, we recognize the importance of fostering partnerships and coalitions with other stakeholders, including governments, non-profit organizations, and civil society groups. By working together towards common goals and shared values, businesses can amplify their impact and drive collective action on pressing social and environmental issues.

Consideration of the employer-employee relationship sheds light on the importance of creating inclusive and equitable workplaces that empower employees to contribute to the greater good.

Businesses that prioritize diversity, inclusion, and employee well-being not only attract top talent but also foster cultures of innovation, creativity, and resilience.

When employees feel valued, respected, and empowered, they are more likely to go above and beyond their duties to make a positive impact on society.

Reflecting on our journey from coercion to collaboration, we recognize that businesses and leaders have a unique opportunity – and indeed, a moral imperative – to leverage their influence for the greater good.

Beyond the pursuit of profit and market share, businesses can create lasting value by addressing the root causes of social and environmental challenges and working towards a more just, equitable, and sustainable world.

As we continue to navigate the complexities of business and leadership, may we remain committed to impacting society at large in meaningful and transformative ways.

How can we each contribute to creating a more just, equitable, and sustainable future for all, and what steps can we take to ensure that our businesses and organizations are forces for positive change in the world?

Chapter 11: Tools for Transformation, Practical Strategies for Change

In this chapter, we equip ourselves with practical tools and strategies to drive meaningful transformation in our lives, organizations, and communities. Building on the insights gained from previous chapters, we explore actionable steps that individuals and leaders can take to create positive change in the world.

1. Cultivating Self-Awareness: The journey of transformation begins with self-awareness – a deep

understanding of our values, beliefs, strengths, and weaknesses.

By reflecting on our experiences, identifying our core values, and acknowledging our blind spots, we lay the foundation for personal growth and development.

2. Setting Clear Intentions: Intentions serve as guiding lights that illuminate our path forward. By setting clear intentions aligned with our values and aspirations, we empower ourselves to take purposeful action and make intentional choices that lead to positive outcomes.

3. Practicing Mindfulness: Mindfulness is the practice of being present and fully engaged in the moment, free from judgment or distraction. By cultivating mindfulness through meditation, breathwork, or other contemplative practices, we develop greater clarity, focus, and resilience in the face of challenges.

4. Building Empathy and Connection: Empathy is the ability to understand and share the feelings of others, fostering deeper connections and mutual understanding. By actively listening, seeking to understand, and empathizing with the experiences of others, we build trust, rapport, and collaboration in our relationships.

5. Leveraging Strengths-Based Leadership: Strengths-based leadership focuses on identifying and leveraging our unique strengths and talents to achieve our goals.

In recognizing and developing our strengths, as well as those of our team members, we create environments where everyone can thrive and contribute their best.

6. Embracing Courageous Conversations: Courageous conversations are honest, respectful dialogues that address difficult topics and confront challenges head-on. We must therefore foster open communication, vulnerability, and trust. In that sense we create spaces for growth, learning, and understanding in our personal and professional relationships.

7. Practicing Inclusive Leadership: Inclusive leadership prioritizes diversity, equity, and inclusion, creating environments where all voices are valued and respected. It is imperative that in order to realize these ideals it requires us embracing diverse perspectives, fostering belonging, and addressing systemic barriers, we create cultures of belonging and innovation where everyone can contribute and succeed.

8. Embodying Servant Leadership: Servant leadership focuses on serving the needs of others, rather than wielding power or authority for personal gain. By putting the needs of others first, leading with humility and empathy, and empowering those around us, we create cultures of trust, collaboration, and shared success.

9. Fostering a Growth Mindset: A growth mindset is the belief that our abilities and intelligence can be developed through effort and perseverance. By embracing challenges, learning from failures, and seeking opportunities for growth and development, we cultivate resilience, adaptability, and lifelong learning.

10. Taking Inspired Action: Transformation requires action – small, consistent steps taken towards our goals and aspirations. By breaking our goals down into manageable tasks, creating action plans, and holding ourselves accountable, we turn our intentions into

reality and create lasting change in our lives and communities.

As we embark on the journey of transformation, may we embrace these practical tools and strategies with openness, curiosity, and a willingness to learn and grow. How can we each incorporate these tools into our daily lives and leadership practices, and what impact can they have on our personal growth and collective well-being?

Chapter 12: The Path to True Liberation, A Call to Action

"What is the true measure of our liberation, and how do we embark on the journey towards it?"

Throughout our exploration, we have journeyed through the complexities of leadership, power dynamics, and societal impact. We have uncovered insights into authentic leadership, collaboration, and the transformative potential of businesses and individuals.

Now, as we stand at the cusp of migrating from a state of ideological suppression to a state of true liberation, we are called to action – to step boldly into our worlds, our spheres and create *the* change we wish to see.

Reflecting on our journey thus far, we recognize that true liberation begins with a deep understanding of ourselves and our values.

It is about embracing our authenticity, stepping into our power, and aligning our actions with our highest ideals. How can we each cultivate a sense of inner freedom and authenticity, and what steps can we take to live in alignment with our true selves?

Moreover, true liberation requires us to recognize and challenge the systems of oppression and inequality that perpetuate injustice and suffering in our world. It is about dismantling barriers, amplifying marginalized voices, and advocating for justice and equity for all. How can we each use our privilege and influence to dismantle systems of oppression and create a more just and equitable world?

As we reflect on our exploration of leadership and collaboration, we recognize that true liberation is not a solitary journey but a collective endeavor. It is about coming together, building coalitions, and working towards common goals and shared values. How can we each contribute to building bridges, fostering understanding, and creating spaces for dialogue and collaboration?

The path to true liberation also requires us to embrace courage and resilience in the face of adversity and uncertainty. It is about standing up for what is right, even when it is difficult or unpopular, and persevering in the face of obstacles and challenges. It is therefore a requirement that we all cultivate courage, resilience, and perseverance in our lives and leadership practices.

Furthermore, true liberation is about fostering a sense of belonging and connection – to ourselves, to each other, and to the world around us.

It is about recognizing the inherent worth and dignity of every individual and creating environments where everyone feels seen, heard, and valued. How can we each foster a sense of belonging and connection in our communities and organizations?

As we embark on the path to true liberation, we are called to action – to be the change we wish to see in the world, to stand up for justice and equality, and to build a more compassionate and inclusive society for all. How can we each take inspired action in our own lives and communities, and what impact can we have on the world around us?

In conclusion, the path to true liberation is a journey of self-discovery, courage, and collective action. It is about embracing our authenticity, challenging oppression, fostering connection, and taking inspired action to create positive change in the world.

As we heed the call to action and embark on this journey together, may we be guided by the wisdom of our hearts, the deep persuasions of our convictions, and the power of our collective will.

Together, we can create a world where all people, irrespective of ethnic background, economic prowess, political, religious or spiritual persuasions are free to thrive and flourish, in harmony with each other and with the planet we call home.